Fables and Folk-Tales

from an Eastern Forest.

I. Rice-fields at the foot of Būkit Perak or Peraḳ (i.e. Silver) Mountain, in the interior of Kedah, Malay Peninsula.

Fables & Folk-Tales

from an Eastern Forest

Collected and Translated by

WALTER SKEAT, M.A., M.R.A.S., F.A.I.,

Sometime Scholar of Christ's College, Cambridge,
late of the Federated Malay States Service,
Author of " Malay Magic."

Illustrated by

F. H. TOWNSEND.

CAMBRIDGE :
At the University Press.
1901

CAMBRIDGE
UNIVERSITY PRESS

32 Avenue of the Americas, New York NY 10013-2473, USA

Cambridge University Press is part of the University of Cambridge.

It furthers the University's mission by disseminating knowledge in the pursuit of education, learning and research at the highest international levels of excellence.

www.cambridge.org
Information on this title: www.cambridge.org/9781107432888

First published 1901
First paperback edition 2014

A catalogue record for this publication is available from the British Library

ISBN 978-1-107-43288-8 Paperback

To

my Friend and Fellow-worker

RICHARD JAMES WILKINSON.

TABLE OF CONTENTS.

Table of Contents

LIST OF ILLUSTRATIONS.

List of Illustrations

N.B. The Tail-pieces represent respectively Small Lizards,
the Tiger, Mouse-deer, Otter, Tortoise, Monitor Lizard,
Wild Bull, Monkey, and Elephant.

INTRODUCTION.

THE Tales contained in this little volume were
taken down from the lips of the Malay
peasantry, in the twilight of their own tropical
jungle, during the progress of the Cambridge Ex-
pedition of 1899 through the remoter States of the
Malay Peninsula. The tales themselves, as will be
obvious to the reader, are the merest gleanings from
an extensive harvest-field, and make no pretensions
whatever to any completeness or finality. For the
most part, indeed, the book is an experiment, the
object of which is to ascertain to what extent the
native " Soother-of-care " (as the village story-teller
is designated by his Malayan audience) may tell his
tale in words of his own choosing, without alienating
the interest of the Western reader.

To save the translation from becoming too
slavishly literal and (consequently) unreadable, the
natural luxuriance of Oriental phraseology has been

kept within limits, but otherwise the originals have been closely adhered to, and the fine art of embellishment has been disregarded. If something has been lost through an occasional want of conformity with Western ideas, it is hoped that much will also be gained in point and quaintness through the more faithful preservation of the original expressions.

The hero of these tales is a small chevrotain which is to be found in almost every part of the jungles of Malaya. It is commonly called the Malayan Mouse-deer; but in spite of its name it belongs rather to the antelope tribe, the heel-bone (os calcis) of its hinder leg projecting in a fashion which I believe is never seen in the true deer. Its eye-teeth, too, are curiously long and projecting, and its hoofs are cloven to an extent which in so small a creature is really remarkable. At the same time it is a most beautiful little animal, with big dark pleading eyes and all the grace and elegance of a gazelle. It is a favourite character in Malayan folk-tales, in which it is credited with such inexhaustible powers of resource and mother-wit that it is often given the name of "Ment'ri B'lukar," the "Vizier of the Underwood" (or "Brush"). No difficulties are too great for it to overcome; no

perils can daunt it; even the savage lords of
Forest-glade and River-pool suffer contumelious
defeat when 'Friend' Mouse-deer is their adversary.
In fact, the place occupied by the Mouse-deer in
Malayan Folk-lore is exactly analogous to the place
occupied by Reynard the Fox in the folk-tales of
Europe, and by Brer Rabbit in the immortal cycle
of tales which take their name from 'Uncle Remus.'

Here, however, it is perhaps worth noting that
although the Mouse-deer as a master of 'slimness'
is given the preeminent place among all the beasts
of the field, its mantle is sometimes temporarily
permitted to fall upon the shoulders of other and
quite different members of the animal creation.
Hence we find in the 14th story, that the King-
crow is worsted by a Water-snail, and I may add
that in a Javanese fable of the same type (for
which compare our own 'Hare-and-Tortoise' Fable)
the Mouse-deer itself plays the part of the deceived,
instead of that of the deceiver.

But the subject of the mutual relations of the
Beasts in Malayan Fable is one which has yet to
be worked 'out, and which lies unfortunately far
beyond the bounds of the present disquisition.

The other animals here introduced to the reader,

for the most part resemble their Indian relatives and require little or no further description from the writer, with the possible exception of the " Wild Bull" which is the *Bos gaurus* or "Gaur" of India; rather than *Bos sondaicus* which is said to have been once or twice reported from the same region.

In making the illustrations which appear in this book, the artist has taken infinite pains for which I should like to take this occasion to thank him; he has certainly made the best of such somewhat scanty material as was available. With a few occasional exceptions, no serious attempt has been made to analyse the stories here given, or to trace their sources[1]. It was felt that to do so would be only to break a butterfly upon a wheel; and the writer prefers that this little book should be to others what it is to him, a delightful memorial of a most fascinating country and people.

W. S.

---

[1] In addition however to a few references given in the notes, I may perhaps mention, for the benefit of local readers, the Malay versions of the " Hikayat P'landok Jinaka" ed. H. C. Klinkert (Leyden, 1885), and the " Sha'ir P'landok" (both of which are lithographed).

FABLES AND FOLK TALES.

FATHER 'LIME-STICK' AND THE FLOWER-PECKER.

OLD Father Lime-stick once limed a tree for birds and caught a Flower-pecker (a small bird about as big as one's thumb). He was just about to kill and eat it when the bird cried out, "O Grandfather, surely you are not going to eat me? Why, flesh, feathers and all, I am no bigger than your thumb!" "What?" said the old man, "do you expect me then to let you go?" "Yes," said the bird, "only let me go, and I will fetch you such a talisman as never was—a Bezoar-stone as big as a coconut and worth at least a thousand." Said the old man, "Do you really mean it?" "Really, I do," replied the bird. "Just let me go, and I'll bring it to you." Then (on being released) he flew off and perched on a tree, and began to preen his feathers, to get rid of the bird-lime. And presently the old man said, "Where has that bird got to? Bird, where is the Bezoar-stone you promised to bring me, the one that was worth at least a thousand?" "Out-on-you," was the reply, "this is really *too* ridiculous. Just think of me, with my body as big as your thumb, carrying a Bezoar-stone as big as a coconut! It really is too absurd. Why, have I even got the strength to lift it?" At this the old man held his peace. "Well," continued the bird, "you will gain nothing by repenting that you set me free. Only remember in future not to undertake an affair quite out of keeping with your own powers. Neither try to get your arms round a tree too big for your embrace, nor attempt to climb one higher than your strength permits you."

THE KING OF THE TIGERS IS SICK.

WHEN the Great King of All the Tigers was sick, the Tiger-Crown-Prince made obeisance and said, "If my Lord will taste of the flesh of every beast of the field peradventure my Lord may recover." So the Great King commanded the Crown-Prince to summon every kind of beast into his presence, and as they appeared the King ate of them. Only the Mouse-deer, who was likewise summoned, refused to appear.

Therefore the great King's wrath was kindled against the Mouse-deer and in the end he too was fain to appear. And when he appeared he was questioned by the King. "Why did you not attend at the first when we had summoned hither every kind of beast that lives in the field?" The Mouse-deer replied, "Your slave could not approach your Majesty because of a dream of certain medicine

3

that would make your Majesty well." The King replied, "What medicine was this of which you dreamed?" "Your slave dreamed that the only remedy for your Majesty's sickness was for your Majesty to seize and devour *That which is Nearest your Majesty*."

Immediately on hearing this the Great King of the Tigers seized the Prince of the Tigers and devoured him also. And straightway the King was cured, and the Mouse-deer himself became Crown-Prince in turn.

THE MOUSE-DEER'S SHIPWRECK.

"COME," said the Mouse-deer to the Stump-tailed Heron, "come and sail with me to Java." So they set sail, and Friend Mouse-deer held the tiller and Friend Heron spread the sail. And the wind blew from the North. Soon however Friend Mouse-deer got drowsy, and let the boat fall out of the wind.

At this Friend Heron said, "Why does the boat fall off? How is your helm, Friend Mouse-deer?" "I was only taking a few winks," said he. "Bring her up to the wind again," said the Heron. And the Mouse-deer replied, "All right. I'm 'on the spot,'" (said he). Presently however he dozed again, and the Heron exclaimed, "Oh, if that's to be it, you may die and be done with. I'll peck a hole in this boat of ours and you'll go to the bottom."

But the Mouse-deer said, "*Please* don't, I'm *such* a bad hand at swimming." So they sailed on. And the Mouse-deer dozed a third time. At this the Heron could contain himself no longer, and said, "Confound you, Friend Mouse-deer, for sleeping at the helm." And losing his temper he pecked a hole in the boat, and the boat let in the water and Friend Heron flew away. But the Mouse-deer swam struggling with his feet in the midst of the sea.

Presently there came up a young Shark who exclaimed, "I'll have a meal off you this time at all events." But the Mouse-deer answered, "What, Friend Shark, you'll make a meal off *me*? why, in place of the little flesh I've got, if you'll carry me ashore, I'll teach you some excellent Magic which will save you from ever having to hunt for your food again." To this the Shark replied, "Agreed. If you'll teach me your 'excellent Magic' I'll carry you ashore." So the Mouse-deer got upon Friend Shark's back, and was carried straight ashore.

And on their arrival the Mouse-deer said, "Wait here a bit, while I go and get the simples."

6

II. "But presently he dragged the Shark up on to the dry beach,
and made butcher's-meat of him."

And going aland he hunted up a rattan (cane) creeper and took it back with him and said, "Now I'll give you the simples I spoke of," and bound it fast to Friend Shark's tail. And presently the Shark said, "Why have you made the line fast to my tail?" But the Mouse-deer replied, "Keep quite quiet till I have tied you up properly, and then I'll give you the simples." But presently he dragged the Shark up on to the dry beach, and made butcher's-meat of him. Just then however a Tiger came up, exclaiming, "Here's really a good meal for Me, for once in a way!" To this, however, the Mouse-deer replied, "What is the use of eating *me*, when there's already plenty of butcher's-meat and to spare?" "Very well, I'll share it with you," said the Tiger. The Mouse-deer replied, "You may share it with me by all means, if you will only go and get some water to do the cooking." So the Tiger went off to get water and presently came back with it.

"Wash the meat before you roast it," said the Mouse-deer. The Tiger took the meat and washed it in the water. "Go and fetch fire and roast it," said the Mouse-deer. The Tiger fetched fire and came back to do the cooking. And when the meat was done, "Now go and fetch some drinking water," said the Mouse-deer, "and we'll have our meal together." So the Tiger went off again to fetch the drinking water. But the Mouse-deer in the meantime made off with the Shark's meat and climbed up with it to the top of a She-oak Tree. And presently the Tiger came back and found both Mouse-deer and meat missing. At this he exclaimed, "For once in a way, Mr Mouse-deer, you've fairly cheated Me; if we don't meet again no matter, but if we do, I'll be the death of you." And here the story ends.

WHO KILLED THE OTTER'S BABIES?
(A 'CLOCK' STORY.)

THE Otter said to the Mouse-deer, "Friend
Mouse-deer, will you be so good as to take
charge of the children till I come back? I am going
down to the river to catch fish, and when I come
back I'll share the takings with you. The Mouse-
deer replied, "Very well! go along, and I'll look
after the children." So the Otter went down to
the river to catch fish.

(Here the story of What the Otter did stops and
the story of What happened when the Woodpecker
sounded the war-gong commences.) The Mouse-
deer was Chief Dancer of the War-dance, and as he
danced, he trod on the Otter's Babies and crushed
them flat. Presently the Otter returned home, bring-
ing a string of fish with him. On arriving he saw
that his children had been killed, and exclaimed,
"How comes it, Friend Mouse-deer, that my Babies

have died?" The Mouse-deer replied, "The Wood-pecker came and sounded the war-gong, and I, being Chief War-Dancer, danced; and forgetting about your children I trod upon them and crushed them flat."

On hearing this the Otter went and made complaint unto King Solomon, prostrating himself and saying, "Your Majesty's most humble slave craves pardon for presuming to address your Majesty, but Friend Mouse-deer has murdered your slave's children, and your slave desires to learn whether he is guilty or not according to the Law of the Land." King Solomon replied, saying, "If the Mouse-deer hath done this thing wittingly, assuredly he is guilty of death." Then he summoned the Mouse-deer before him.

And when the Mouse-deer came into the presence of the King, the King enquired of the Otter, "What is your charge against him?" The Otter replied, "Your slave accuses him of the murder of your slave's children; your slave would hear the Law of the Land." Then the King said unto the Mouse-deer, "Was it your doing that the Otter's children were killed?" The Mouse-deer replied,

III. "Presently the Otter returned home," . . . and "saw that his children had been killed."

"Assuredly it was, but I crave pardon for doing so."
"How was it then," said the King, "that you came
to kill them?" The Mouse-deer replied, "Your
slave came to kill them because the Woodpecker
appeared and sounded the war-gong. Your slave,
as your Majesty is aware, is Chief Dancer
of the War-dance, therefore your slave danced,
and forgetting about the Otter's children, your
slave trod upon them and crushed them flat."
Here the King sent for the Woodpecker also,
and the Woodpecker came before him. "Was it
you, Woodpecker," said the King, "who sounded
the war-gong?" "Assuredly it was," said the
Woodpecker,—"forasmuch as your slave saw the
Great Lizard wearing his sword." The King
replied, "If that is the case, there is no fault
to be found in the Woodpecker" (for the Woodpecker was Chief Beater of the War-gong).
Then the King commanded the Great Lizard to
be summoned, and when he arrived, the King
enquired, "Was it you, Lizard, who were wearing
your sword?" The Great Lizard replied, "Assuredly
it was, your Majesty." "And why were you wearing your sword?" The Great Lizard replied,

"Your slave wore it forasmuch as your slave saw that the Tortoise had donned his coat of mail." So the Tortoise was summoned likewise. "Why did you, Tortoise, don your coat of mail?" The Tortoise replied, "Your slave donned it forasmuch as your slave saw the King-crab trailing his three-edged pike." Then the King-crab was sent for. "Why were you, King-crab, trailing your three-edged pike?" "Because your slave saw that the Crayfish had shouldered his lance." Then the King sent for the Crayfish and said, "Was it you, Crayfish, who were shouldering your lance?" And the Crayfish replied, "Assuredly it was, your Majesty." "And why did you shoulder it?" "Because your slave saw the Otter coming down to devour your slave's own children." "Oh," said King Solomon, "if that is the case, you, Otter, are the guilty party and your complaint of your children's death cannot be sustained against the Mouse-deer by the Law of the Land."

A VEGETARIAN DISPUTE.

ONCE upon a time Jágong the Maize-plant made boast, and said, " If Rice should cease to exist, I alone should suffice to sustain Mankind." But Dāgun the Liane and Gādong the Jungle Yam each made a like boast, and as the parties could not agree, the case was brought before King Solomon. Said Solomon, " All three of you are perfectly right, albeit it were perhaps better that Jágong should sustain Mankind because of his comrade-ship with Káchang the Bean." Thereat the wrath of Dāgun the Liane and Gādong the Yam waxed hot against Jágong, and they went off together to hunt for a fruit-spike of the Jungle Fig-tree, whereon to impale him, but found none. And meanwhile Jágong hearing news of their quest, set to work to find Arrow-poison. And when he had

13

found it he poisoned Gādong therewith (wherefore to this day the Jungle Yam has narcotic properties). Then Gādong the Yam being wroth thereat speared Jágong in turn (wherefore to this day the cobs of Maize are perforated). And Jágong reaching out in turn seized the pointed shoot of a 'Wilang' stem and wounded Dāgun therewith.

At this juncture the parties to the quarrel went before the Prophet Elias, who said, "This matter is too great for me, take ye it before Solomon." And Solomon said, "Let them fight it out between them, that the rage of their hearts may be appeased." Wherefore there was battle between them for twice seven days. Now Māta Lémbu the 'Ox-eye' Tree stood nigh to watch the battle, and its skin was grazed by bullets (whereof its bark still shows the scars). But the 'Pĕrāchak' Shrub on the other hand was filled with fear, and instead of drawing nearer, in order to see the battle, it stood upon tiptoe (wherefore it still grows long and lanky). But 'Ándram' the sedge was the most afraid and ran to a place afar off, but as it still heard the noise of battle it plunged into the river (wherefore to this day it grows over the surface of water).

from an Eastern Forest

And when the twice seven days were ended, the battle being still undecided, the combatants were parted, and a space was set between them by Solomon. And Gădong the Yam made he to sit down, and Dāgun the Liane to lie down. But Jágong the Maize-plant and Káchang the Bean he made to stand together.

THE FRIENDSHIP OF THE SQUIRREL AND
THE CREEPING FISH.

FROM the beginning Tūpai the Squirrel and
Rūan the Creeping Fish were ever close and
faithful friends. And one day Tūpai's wife fell sick
and Tūpai enquired of the Medicine-man what
medicine he should give her, and the Medicine-man
prescribed the egg of a fowl. But Tūpai could not
by any means obtain it. Therefore he told Rūan
the Fish of his trouble, and Rūan promised to help
him, if he had to die for it. Next morning
therefore Rūan swam into a bamboo water-tube
which a woman was filling in the river and was
carried back inside it to the house, where it was left
leaning against the house-wall close to the roosting-
place of the fowls. And at evening Rūan crept
out of the tube and taking into his mouth an egg
out of a hen's nest carried it back with him into the
tube again. Next morning the woman once more
took the water-tube down to the river to fill it.

16

IV. "And presently he looked out and bit through the stalk of the coconut so that it fell into the river."

Then Rūan swam out of the tube into the river again and brought the egg rejoicing to his friend Tūpai. And the Squirrel's wife on receiving the egg immediately recovered.

Another day Rūan's wife fell ill and the Medicine-man prescribed the heart of a crocodile, but Rūan likewise had no means of obtaining it. Therefore Tūpai the Squirrel bit a hole in a coconut growing on a palm which overhung the river and crept inside it. And presently he looked out and bit through the stalk of the coconut so that it fell into the river and was swallowed by a crocodile, Tūpai himself lying coiled inside it. And presently he crept out of the coconut into the crocodile's stomach, and bit out its heart. And the crocodile struggled greatly till it came to the shore and died there. Then the Squirrel crept out of the crocodile's jaws and gave the heart to Rūan the Fish. And Rūan's wife recovered immediately also.

THE PELICAN'S PUNISHMENT.

UNDAN the Pelican being hungry told Rūan
the Fish that his pool would shortly dry up,
and offered to carry himself or any members of
his family to another pool to see how they
liked it.

To this Rūan agreed; and Undan carried him
over to the pool and back again as stipulated, and
the fish liking it informed all his relatives.

Then Undan carried the fish back again to the
new pool and returned to fetch the rest of his
family. But instead of putting them into the
pool, Undan sat in a tree and ate the fish till his
droppings reached to the lower branches.

By this time there were no more fish to be

eaten and Undan commenced in like manner to
cheat the family of Kĕtam the Crab. But as soon
as ever Kĕtam caught sight of the droppings he
saw through the trick and pinched Undan's neck
so that he died.

THE TIGER GETS HIS DESERTS.

A TIGER which had been caught in a trap seeing a man, begged to be released. The man said to the Tiger, "If I let you out of the trap will you promise not to attack me?" "Certainly," said the Tiger, and the man therefore let the Tiger go, but the moment the Tiger was loose it sprang upon the man and caught him. At this the man begged the Tiger to wait until he had enquired how the law stood with reference to their contract, and the Tiger agreed to do so. The man and the Tiger therefore set out together; and on coming to a Road the man said, "O Road, Road, is it lawful to requite evil for good, or good for good only?" The Road replied, "I do good to mankind, but they requite me with evil, defiling (my surface) as they go." Then they came to a Tree, of which the man asked the same question. The Tree replied,

V. "On reaching the trap, he requested the Tiger to 'Step inside'."

"I do good to mankind, but they requite me with evil, lopping off my branches and cutting me down." At the last they came to the Mouse-deer and the man made the same enquiry as before. The Mouse-deer replied, "I must really go into the question thoroughly before I answer it; let us go back together to the trap." On reaching the trap, he requested the Tiger to "Step inside," and the Tiger entering the trap, the Mouse-deer let down the door of the trap, and exclaimed, "Accursed Brute, you have returned evil for good and now you shall die for it." He then called in the neighbours and had the Tiger killed.

THE TIGER'S MISTAKE.

A MAN was taking his little boy home through the jungle near the headwaters of the Lĕbih River in the interior of Kĕlántan, when they were overtaken by night. The boy was frightened and said to his father, "Father, I am so frightened, let me sleep in the middle." The father replied, "How can you sleep in the middle seeing there are but two of us?" Nevertheless the boy replied, "Father, I *must* sleep in the middle"; and the father to pacify him took the boy's head in his lap, and they went to sleep together on the bank of the river. Now Rīmau the Tiger came that way and beheld a man with four arms and four legs and only a single head. Rīmau was astonished at this, and went to Buáya the Old Crocodile in the bight and said, "Friend Buáya, there is a human being asleep on the bank who has four arms and four legs and only a single

22

VI. "Rīmau being startled leaped backwards and fell into the river, where he was himself devoured by the Crocodile according to his compact."

head." At this old Buáya laughed consumedly and said, "What nonsense is this? Go and snuff round about the body and you will soon find it has two heads rather than one. Whatever you seize shall be your portion, but whatever plunges into the river (to escape) shall be mine."

So Rīmau went back to snuff round the body, and as he was snuffing his whiskers tickled the man's nostrils and the man sneezed very violently. And at this Rīmau being startled leaped backwards and fell into the river, where he was himself devoured by the Crocodile according to his compact.

THE TUNE THAT MAKES THE
TIGER DROWSY.

THERE is a tune which when played upon the
"Kĕrōtong" (a two-stringed bamboo harp)
makes Rīmau the Tiger drowsy, but only a few
old people know it. One evening two men were
sitting together and playing in a hut in the jungle
when two tigers overheard them.

The tigers took counsel together, and one of
them said to the other, "You shall be the first to
go into the house; Whatever you seize shall therefore be your portion, but Whatever plunges down
the steps (to escape) shall be mine." At this the
second tiger ascended the house-ladder and was just
crouching upon the topmost rung when one of the
men to amuse himself commenced to play the

24

Tune that makes the Tiger Drowsy. As soon as the Tiger heard it he began to grow sleepy, and presently fell plump down the steps to the ground, where he was seized by his companion. And when he objected, his companion exclaimed, "Did we not agree that Whatever plunged down the steps was to be my portion?" and proceeded to devour him at his leisure.

THE "TIGERS' FOLD."

THERE is a place called Ūlu Sĕtiu' in the
country of Trenggānu, where the Tigers are
penned in a fold called "Kándang Bālok." Within
this Fold there are two lakes or ponds. By swimming through one of these ponds (on setting out
for a journey) the Tigers turn themselves into men,
and by swimming through the other (on their
return) they change themselves back into Tigers[1].
For within the Fold itself the Tigers always retain
the shape of beasts, with the exception of the Tiger-
chief who always appears in the form of a man. It
is this Chief whom men call by the name of The
' Tiger Devil ' or ' Tiger Demon[2]' and who enters

[1] According to some accounts of the Malays the Tigers have
a regular form of Government and a town of their own, the
houses of which have their framework made of human bones
and are thatched with women's hair.

[2] " Pong Mor " or Hantu Bĕlian.

26

into the bodies of sorcerers when they invoke the Tiger Spirit. A sorcerer in a trance was once in former days seized by this Tiger-chief, who slung him across his shoulder and carried him off to the Tigers' Fold. On reaching the Fold, however, the Tiger-chief kept the sorcerer for safety in his own house, which was built upon four posts of extraordinary height. From this position the sorcerer beheld the baffled herd of hungry tigers who prowled around the posts of the house when they smelt the smell of a man, although they did not dare to attack it for fear of their Chief. For seven days and seven nights the sorcerer was thus imprisoned, but he then succeeded in making his escape, and on returning to his family he related all that he had seen and heard in the Fold of the Tigers.

THE TIGER AND THE SHADOW.

THERE was a "salt-lick" in the jungle to which all the beasts of the forest resorted, but they were greatly afraid by reason of an old Tiger which killed one of them every day. At length, therefore, P'lando' the Mouse-deer said to the Tiger, "Why not permit me to bring you a beast every day, to save you from hunting for your food?" The Tiger consented and P'lando' went off to make arrangement with the beasts. But he could not persuade any of them to go, and after three days he set off, taking nobody with him but Kuwis the smallest of the Flying Squirrels. On their arrival P'lando' said to the Tiger, "I could not bring you any of the other beasts because the way was blocked by a fat old Tiger with a Flying Squirrel sitting astride its muzzle." On hearing this the Tiger exclaimed, "Let us go and find it and drive it

28

VII. "On hearing this, the Tiger sprang into the river to attack his own shadow, and was drowned immediately."

away." The three therefore set out, the Flying Squirrel perched upon the Tiger's muzzle and the Mouse-deer sitting astride upon its hind quarters. On reaching the river, the Mouse-deer pointed to the Tiger's likeness in the water and exclaimed, "Look there! That is the fat old Tiger that I saw." On hearing this, the Tiger sprang into the river to attack his own shadow, and was drowned immediately.

WIT WINS THE DAY.

P'LANDO' the Mouse-deer went to look for the Wild Bull of the Clearing[1] and said to him, "The Bull of the Young Bush is exceedingly wroth against you, and is using most foul and opprobrious language." Then he went to the Wild Bull of the Young Bush[2], and said to him likewise, "The Bull of the Clearing is saying all manner of insulting things about you." (For he wanted to set them on to fight together.)

Next day they each set out and met upon the boundary between the Cleared Land and the Young Bush. And when they charged down upon each other, the Bull of the Young Bush was slain by the Bull of the Clearing, the Mouse-deer sitting upon an ant-hill to excite them to the combat.

[1] Sĕladang Chĕrang.
[2] Sĕladang B'lūkar.

30

VIII. "The Bull of the Young Bush was slain by the Bull of the Clearing, the
Mouse-deer sitting upon an ant-hill to excite them to the combat."

But during the battle the white ants extended their burrows into the Mouse-deer's back as he sat on the ant-hill, so that he could not get up again. Therefore he said to the survivor, "If you have the strength, Friend Bull, do me the favour to scatter this ant-hill." At this the Bull of the Clearing scattered the ant-hill with his horns and scampered off (to escape from the ants). So the Mouse-deer cut the throat of the Bull of the Young Bush (according to the Muhammedan rites) and began to flay the skin from the carcase.

At this moment Rīmau the Tiger appeared and said, "Will you share your meat with me?" And the Mouse-deer said, "By all means." But when he had finished flaying, rain began to fall, and the Mouse-deer ordered the Tiger to cut him some prickly boughs (with which to make a shelter from the rain)—boughs of the "Rīseh," and boughs of the "Túnggal dūri." The Tiger did so and slung them across his shoulder to carry them home, but the river bank was very slippery and his shoulders were smeared all over with blood as he kept trying to clamber on to the raft.

Just then, seeing the Mouse-deer, he asked,

31

"What in the world makes you shiver so, Friend Mouse-deer?" The Mouse-deer replied (in ferocious tones), "I am quivering with anticipation!" and the Tiger, thinking that the Mouse-deer had designs upon himself, became so nervous that he plunged into the river, and left the meat to the Mouse-deer.

THE KING-CROW AND THE WATER-SNAIL.

A WATER-SNAIL was coming up-stream from the lower reaches, when a King-crow heard it. Said the King-crow to himself, "Who can it be coming up-stream, that exclaims so loudly at the rapids? One might say it was a man, but that there is nothing to be seen." So the King-crow settled on a tree to watch, but as he could see nothing from his perch on the tree he flew down to the ground, and walked along by the water-side. And when he thought to see some man exclaiming, he caught sight of the Water-snail.

"Hullo, you there," said he, "where do you come from?" "I come from the eddy below the rapids," said the Water-snail, "and I only want to get as far as the head-waters of this river." Said the King-crow, "Wait a bit. Suppose you go down to the river-mouth as quickly as you can and we will have a wager on it." (Now rivers are the Water-snail's domain, in which he has many comrades.)

"What is to be the stake?" asked the Water-snail. "If I am beaten I will be your slave, and look after your aroids[1] and wild calladiums[2]" (on which the Water-snails feed). Then the King-crow asked, "And what will *you* stake?" The Water-snail replied, "If I am beaten, the river shall be handed over to you and you shall be King of the River." But the Water-snail begged for a delay of twice seven days, saying that he felt knocked up after ascending the rapids. And the delay was granted accordingly.

Meanwhile however the Water-snail hunted up a great number of his friends and instructed them to conceal themselves in each of the higher reaches of the river, and to reply immediately when the King-crow challenged them.

[1] Birah.
[2] Kĕmahang.

34

The day arrived, and the King-crow flew off, and in each of the higher reaches the Water-snail's friends replied to the challenge. And at the river-mouth the Water-snail replied in person. So the King-crow was defeated and has ever since remained the slave of the Water-snail.

FATHER 'FOLLOW-MY-NOSE' AND THE FOUR PRIESTS.

OLD Father 'Follow-my-nose,' he *would* walk straight. When he came to a house he would climb over the house, and when he came to a tree he would climb over the tree. So one day he came to a ' Jĕrai ' tree, and after climbing up it (on the one side) he was commencing to climb down the branches (on the other) when he was observed by four Priests of the Yellow Robe.

"If you try to get down *that* way, you'll inevitably fall and kill yourself," was the caution given by the Yellow-Robes, and they forthwith proceeded to spread out one of their Yellow Robes to catch him in, each of the four Priests holding it by one corner.

Father ' Follow-my-nose ' however threw himself down without a moment's warning, and the heads of the four Priests were violently dashed together so that they all four immediately broke their own pates.

36

Old Father Follow-my-nose himself, however, took no sort of harm, and so without turning aside he went on till he reached the hut of an aged crone dwelling on the outskirts of a village. Here he halted while the crone went out to pick up the bodies of the four Priests and bring them back with her to the hut. And presently an opium-eater passed, and the crone called out to him, "Hullo, Mr Opium-Eater, if you'll bury me this 'Yellow-Robe' here, I'll give you a dollar." To this the opium-eater agreed and took the body away to bury it. But when he came back for his money he found the second Priest's body awaiting him, and said to himself "The fellow must have come to life again," and took it away to bury it. Twice again this same thing happened, and so the bodies of all the four Priests were buried. But by the time the last was buried it was broad daylight, and the opium-eater was afraid to go back again for his money.

THE ELEPHANT PRINCESS AND THE PRINCE.

THE Prophet Adam quarrelled with the Lady Eve and they declared they would live apart from each other. Then Adam having taken up his abode by the sea-coast produce the Great Demon (who is known by many different names). But the Lady Eve crossed the sea, making a bridge of a Soap-vine stem (which had grown across the Straits) and became Queen of the People on the Other Side. There she gave birth to a daughter who was called the Youngest Princess. When this Princess grew up, the Queen warned her that if ever she crossed the water she must on no account harry the fields of cane or maize or bananas belonging to the People on the Other Side. One day however the Princess crossed over by means of the Soap-vine stem, and forgetting her mother's warning she harried the fields of the Other People, and was immediately transformed into an Elephant. In this guise she was encountered by a young

38

Prince who was studying at a Monastery near by, and the latter, seeing the great beast in his path, struck her in the centre of the forehead with his iron-shod pike so that the point broke off short in the skin. On reaching home he reported the affair to the Head of his Monastery, saying that he had met a powerful beast of great size which had a tail at each end. The Head however, being a wise man, knew from his account that it was a Princess in disguise, and allowed the young man to set out to find her again. Presently the Prince came to the sea-shore, and in order to cross over the Straits he scooped out the contents of a giant gourd, and seating himself inside it, and, guiding himself by the Soap-vine stem, he reached the other side in safety. On his arrival he made enquiry and was told that the Queen's daughter was sick. Offering his services as a physician he obtained entry into the Palace, where he was shown the Princess, with his iron pike-head still buried in her forehead. He then asked the Queen to erect on the sea-shore a Chamber like a Royal Audience-Hall, and at the same time to build him a big sailing-vessel whose beak should protrude into the Chamber. When this was done the Princess was carried into the Chamber; and the Prince having entered in secret plucked out the iron point from her forehead so that she fell into a swoon. The iron pike-head he concealed in a bamboo tube, and exhibiting the Princess to her family as she lay in a dead faint, he brought her back to life by whistling and patting her; and when she came to, he caused her to be carried home in procession. For this service he received the Princess's hand. After living for some years in happiness with her he wished to revisit his own country; and the Princess accompanied him, taking with her a train of thirty-nine attendants. Before the Princess departed the Queen repeated her former warning, but the Princess again disregarding it was turned back into an elephant, both she, and all her attendants with her.

THE ELEPHANT HAS A BET WITH
THE TIGER.

IN the beginning Gājah the Elephant and Rīmau the Tiger were sworn friends. But one day they came to a clearing and presently encountered Lōtong, the long-tailed Spectacle-monkey. And when he saw the Monkey the Elephant said, "Mr Lōtong yonder is far too noisy; let us try and shake him off; if he falls to me I am to eat you; and if he falls to you, you are to eat me—we will make a wager of it." The Tiger said, "Agreed?" and the Elephant replied, "Agreed." "Very well!" said the Tiger; "you shall try and menace him first." So the Elephant tried to menace the Monkey. "AU! AU! AU!" he trumpeted, and each time he trumpeted the Monkey was scared. But the Monkey went jumping head foremost

S.   41   6

through the branches and never fell to the ground at all.

Presently, therefore, the Tiger asked the Elephant, "Well, Friend Elephant, would you like to try your luck again?" But the Elephant said, "No, thank you. It shall be your turn now; and if he falls to you, you shall eat me—if you really can make him fall!" Then the Tiger went and roared his longest and loudest, and shortened his body as for a spring and growled and menaced the Monkey thrice. And the Monkey leaped and fell at the Tiger's feet, for his feet and hands were paralysed and would not grip the branches any more. Then the Tiger said, "Well, Friend Elephant, I suppose I may eat you now." But the Elephant said, "You have, I admit, won the wager; but I beg you to grant me just seven days' respite, to enable me to visit my wife and children and to make my will." The Tiger granted the request, and the Elephant went home, bellowing and sobbing every foot of the way.

Now the Elephant's wife heard the sound of her husband's voice, and said to her children, "What can be the matter with your Father that he keeps

sobbing so?" And the children listened to make
sure and said, "Yes, it really is Father's voice,
the sobbing, and not that of anybody else."
Presently Father Elephant arrived, and Mother
Elephant asked, "What were you sobbing for,
Father? What have you done to yourself?"
Father Elephant replied, "I made a wager with
Friend Tiger about shaking down a Monkey, and
Friend Tiger beat me; I menaced the Monkey,
but he did not fall; if he had fallen to me, I
was to have eaten Friend Tiger, but if he fell
to Friend Tiger, Friend Tiger was to eat me. I
was beaten, and now Friend Tiger says he is going
to eat me. So I begged leave to come home and
see you, and he has given me just seven days'
respite."

Now for the seven days Father Elephant
kept sobbing aloud, and neither ate nor slept.
And the thing came to the hearing of Friend
Mouse-deer. "What can be the matter with
Friend Elephant that he keeps bellowing and
bellowing, neither does he sleep, so that night is
turned into day, and day into night? What on
earth is the matter with him? Suppose I go and

see " (said the Mouse-deer). Then the Mouse-deer went to see what was wrong, and asked, "What is the matter with you, Friend Elephant, that we hear you bellowing and bellowing every single day and every single night, just now, too, when the Rains are upon us? You are far too noisy."

But the Elephant said, "It is no mere empty noise, Friend Mouse-deer, I have got into a dreadful scrape." "What sort of a scrape?" enquired the Mouse-deer. "I made a wager with Friend Tiger about shaking down a Monkey, and he beat me." "What was the stake?" asked the Mouse-deer. "The stake was that Friend Tiger might eat me if Friend Tiger frightened it down; and if I frightened it down, I might eat Friend Tiger. It fell to Friend Tiger, and now Friend Tiger wants to eat me. And my reason for not eating or sleeping any more is that I have got only just seven days' respite to go home and visit my wife and children and to make my will." Then the Mouse-deer said, "If it came to Friend Tiger's eating you, I should feel exceedingly sorrowful, exceedingly distressed : but things being only as you say, I feel neither." "If you will assist me, I will become your slave, and my descendants shall be your slaves for ever." "Very well, if that is the case, I will assist you," said the Mouse-deer. "Go and look for a jar-full of molasses." Friend Elephant promised to do so, and went to look for it at the house of a maker of Palm-wine. The owner of the house fled for his life, and the jar fell into Friend Elephant's possession, who bore it back to the Mouse-deer.

Then Friend Mouse-deer said, "When does your promise expire?" and Friend Elephant replied, "To-morrow." So when next morning arrived they started, and the Mouse-deer said, "Now pour the molasses over your back and let it spread and spread and run down your legs." Friend Elephant did as he was ordered. Friend Mouse-deer then instructed the Elephant as follows: "As soon as I begin to lick up the molasses on your back, bellow as loud as you can and make believe to be hurt, and writhe and wriggle this way and that."

And presently Friend Mouse-deer commenced to lick hard, and Friend Elephant writhed and wriggled and made believe to be hurt, and made a prodigious noise of trumpeting. In this way they

45

proceeded and Friend Mouse-deer got up and sat astride upon Friend Elephant's back. And the Elephant trumpeted and trumpeted all the way till they met with Friend Tiger. At this Friend Mouse-deer exclaimed, "A single Elephant is very short commons; if I could only catch that big and fat old Tiger there, it would be just enough to satisfy my hunger."

Now when Friend Tiger heard these words of the Mouse-deer, he said to himself, "So I suppose if you catch me, you'll eat me into the bargain, will you?" And Friend Tiger stayed not a moment longer, but fled for his life, fetching very lofty bounds.

And soon he met with the Black Ape, and Friend Ape asked, "Why running so hard, Friend Tiger? Why so much noise, and why, just when the Rains are upon us, too, do you go fetching such lofty bounds?" Friend Tiger replied, "What do you mean by 'so much noise'? What was the Thing that was got upon Friend Elephant's back, that had caught Friend Elephant and was devouring him so that he went writhing and wriggling for the pain of it, and the blood went streaming

46

IX. "And Friend Elephant writhed and wriggled and made believe to be hurt,
and made a prodigious noise of trumpeting."

down in floods? Moreover the Thing that was got on Friend Elephant's back said, to my hearing, that a single Elephant was very short commons: but if It could catch a fat old Tiger like myself that would be just enough to satisfy Its hunger." Friend Ape said, "What was that Thing, Friend Tiger?" "I don't know," said the Tiger. "Ah," mused the Ape, "I wonder if it *could* be Friend Mouse-deer!" "Certainly not," said the Tiger; "why, how in the world could Friend Mouse-deer swallow *Me*? To say nothing of his not being used to meat food" (said he). "Come and let us go back again."

Then they went back again to find the Elephant, and first the Ape went the faster, and then the Tiger went the faster, and then the Ape got in front again. But Friend Mouse-deer sitting on Friend Elephant's back saw them coming and shouted, "Hullo, Father Ape" (said he), "this is a dog's trick indeed; you promise to bring me two tigers and you only bring me one. I refuse to accept it, Father Ape."

Now when Friend Tiger heard this, he ran off at first as fast as he could, but presently he slackened his pace and said, "It is too bad of you, Friend Ape, for trying to cozen me, in order to pay your own debts. For shame! Father Ape! It was only through good luck that he refused to accept me; if he had accepted, I should have been dead and done with. So now, if you come down to the ground, you shall die the death yourself, just for your trying to cheat me." Thus the Tiger and the Ape were set at enmity, and to this day the Tiger is very wroth with the Ape for trying to cheat him. And here the story ends.

PRINCESS SĀDONG OF THE CAVES, WHO REFUSED HER SUITORS.

IF you ever get lost in the Jungle for two or three days together, you will come to a country called " What-you-will." In the chief town of What-you-will there is a royal Pleasure-garden of extraordinary size in which you may see growing many wonderful trees such as the Tree Sugar-cane and the Sweet Lemon. There you will see the tracks of Little People but none of Grown-ups. There too you may hear the noise of great mirth and merriment, but will see nothing till late at night when everybody is asleep; then the Little People come out to amuse themselves with singing and dancing and act the story of Sagembang. Very pleasant it is to see, but everyone who owns rice-fields near by has to use plenty of magic to keep the Little People from stealing his rice.

Here is the country of Princess Sādong, in whose charge are all the caves and hollows of the Limestone Hills. She it was who was born from the big stem of Bamboo and who rules over the Little People, as well as over the wild Hill-goats.

A Prince named Raja Saga first fell very much in love with Princess Sādong, but when he pressed his suit she told him she would marry nobody who did not possess the White Blood (which only belongs to royalty of pure descent).

Now Raja Saga could not pretend to possess this mark of pure descent, and so he received his dismissal and his heart was broken so that he died.

Afterwards the Prince who was born in the Foam asked Princess Sādong to marry him, but the Princess refused him also. Moreover she lost her temper and scratched his forehead with the point of her dagger, so that he fled to a far country. Here he settled, and after many years became a powerful Monarch, but he could not forget Princess Sādong, and so he returned to her country and besought an audience. Now when the Princess saw him she recognised him by the scar upon his brow, and commanded one of her Body-guard to kill him, and thus the Foam-prince died also.

THE SAINT THAT WAS SHOT OUT
OF HIS OWN CANNON.

THE Raja of Patāni ordered Che Long to cast a couple of cannon. The first one was cast successfully, but the second one at every attempt cracked in pieces. At length the Raja told Che Long (the workman) that if he could not succeed in casting it at the next trial, he should die the death. Che Long replied, " I will cast it then at all costs," and in despair of saving his life, he uttered a vow and said, " So my Raja's pleasure be fulfilled, may I take the place of a cannon-ball and be shot out of my own gun." As soon as the words were uttered the casting succeeded and " Che Long " entering the gun caused it to be fired. The charge was exploded in front of the Palace gate at Grésik and Che Long only fell to earth when he reached the village at Kuála Bárat six miles away. Here his remains received burial, and a shrine was built and called by the name of The

Saint of the Western River-mouth. Now in the meanwhile the two guns were put on board ship to be conveyed to Bangkok, and on the way they were both discharged, one of them called the Luck of Patāni emitting a great roar and enveloping the whole country in smoke. This gun is still to be seen at Bangkok. But the other one fell overboard between Tĕlok Tĕngar and Sābor, and was lost. And up to this day vows are paid at the Tomb of Che Long, especially for the recovery of lost or straying cattle, whose milk when the cattle are recovered is offered at the tomb. And in the case of lost or straying cattle, the Patāni folk say, "Fool me not, Grandfather, but point out to me where my cattle are, and if you do so I'll make a pilgrimage to your tomb."

THE SAINTS WHOSE GRAVE-STONES MOVED.

TO' Panjang or "Father Lanky" (as he is generally called) was one of the earliest apostles of Islam in the State of Pătāni and enjoyed a great reputation. At length however Sah Nyāya the Unjust King came to the throne and requested To' Panjang to assist in casting some cannon, the copper being placed in his charge for the purpose. But one day a foreign merchant came to visit him and begged for a portion of the copper, which the Saint gave him, intending no harm thereby. Taxed by the Raja with stealing his copper, To' Panjang admitted his mistake and was condemned to die the death. A pupil of his own was chosen to execute the sentence, but refused to do so, whereupon both master and pupil were strangled[1] and their bodies thrown into the Patāni River, which then escaped to the sea in the neighbourhood of Jámbu. But when they were thrown into the river the two corpses[2] instead of sinking stood miraculously upright in the water, and in this position travelled continually against the stream, both at flood and ebb. At length however the Raja commanded the remains of both saints to be buried ashore, but as often as the bodies were measured for their shrouds, so often they kept outgrowing them. At length therefore a goat was sacrificed and the shrouds having then been measured again were at last found to be of the correct length. The burial therefore was completed; but up to this day the grave-stones of both saints continue to make miraculous movements in proof of the divine nature of To' Panjang and his pupil.

These two tombs are very potent shrines and they lie about two or three miles along Patāni Point.

[1] According to another version, they were both beheaded.

[2] According to another version (though I cannot say, a more likely one) it was the granite grave-stones which miraculously floated and which ever since have continued to move (by way of mute protest, it may be supposed, against the high-handed action of the Unjust King), even when set at rest ashore.

The grave-stones at head and foot are usually found to be about ten feet apart, but it is customary to measure the distance between them twice running in order to take omens as to the length of one's future life. The second measurement always comes different from the first; but if the second measurement proves to be the longer, one's future life will be long in the like proportion.

NAKHŌDA RÁGAM WHO WAS PRICKED TO DEATH BY HIS WIFE'S NEEDLE.

SHIP-MASTER Rágam was the master of a Malay merchant-vessel, and one day he sailed from Jĕring taking with him his beautiful wife Che Sītī of whom he was very fond. On the way she was annoyed by her husband's incessant embraces and warned him to be more careful, reminding him that she was sewing, and remarking how unlucky it was to indulge in such gallantries at sea. Such was his infatuation however that he paid no heed to her warnings, and as he was attempting once more to embrace her, she pricked him to the heart with her needle so that he died.

When she saw that her husband was dead she was alarmed, and shut up the dead body in the deck-house, and whenever any of the crew asked questions, she said, "The master has fever." But when they reached Jĕring, she buried the remains at Bánggor, and the spirit of Nakhōda Rágam entered the body of an old crocodile.

That is why it is still the custom, whenever a big crocodile appears in these parts, for folk to say, "Nakhōda Rágam, your grandchildren beg leave to pass," when he will immediately disappear beneath the surface.

THE LEGEND OF PATĀNI.

THERE once lived, in the interior of Rāman (a province of Patāni), a King of the Fairies who had a beautiful daughter named Princess Nang Cháyang. This Fairy Princess was first of all born in a cave, but the old astrologer prophesied evil of her and said, " This infant must never be kept ashore, set her adrift on the water." Therefore a feast of purification was held in the land, and the Fairy Princess was thrown into the river to drown. Instead of drowning however she rose to the surface, and floated down the river, resting on a mass of foam. As she floated down she was rescued by Rāja Siung, the Tusky Prince. He was called the Tusky Prince because he ate men's flesh till his eye-teeth developed

59

into tusks like those of a cannibal[1]. For once when a follower of his had taken the carcase of a slain goat (which was to be roasted for the Prince) down to the river, to scour it, a vulture flew down while his back was turned, and carried off the goat's heart. The young man feared to take back the flesh without the heart, therefore he slew a boy who was passing by and forced into the goat's carcase the heart of his victim. So the Prince partook of the boy's heart, and when he had eaten it, he rejoiced and said, "This is a better goat's heart than any I have tasted. Why is it so much sweeter than that of other goats I have eaten?" At first the youth said nothing, but afterwards he confessed that it was the heart of a boy. So the Prince commanded to slay a boy daily, in order that he might eat the heart thereof. Wherefore his tusks grew like those of a cannibal, two at top and two at bottom.

Now when Rāja Siung had rescued Princess

---

[1] It is interesting to note in this connection that one of the old Sanskrit names for the Tiger was "Chatur-danta" or the "Four-Toothed" (animal). This epithet applies of course to the four big canines or eye-teeth which are so prominent a characteristic of the Tiger (though found in many other animals).

Nang Cháyang he brought her up in his own palace. And one day when he was hunting in the Jungle he heard the voice of a child, and going to the spot he found a male infant within the hollow stem of a big Bamboo which had been riven open by the wind. This infant he adopted also, and brought up the two children together. And one day when they were sitting on his knees and playing, each of them by accident[1] pulled out a pair of the tusks. And when the Princess grew up, she married Prince Samura Muda. But the boy was ancestor of the Rājas of Rāman, who may not partake of the young Bamboo shoots, because their ancestor came out of the Bamboo before ever they entered Islam.

[1] This explains why the tusks have disappeared in the Rāja of Rāman's descendants.

A MALAYAN DELUGE.

IN the beginning the country of Kĕlántan contained eighteen hundred souls. But one day a great Feast was made for a Circumcision, and all manner of beasts were pitted to fight against each other. There were fights between elephants and fights between buffaloes and fights between bullocks and fights between goats, and at the last there were fights between dogs and cats.

And when the fights took place between dogs and cats a great Flood came down from the mountains, and overwhelmed the people that dwelt in the plains. And they were all drowned in that flood, save only some two or three menials who had been sent up into the Hills to collect firewood.

from an Eastern Forest

Then the sun, moon and stars were extinguished, and there was a great darkness. And when light returned, there was no land but a great sea, and all the habitations of man had been overwhelmed.

KING SOLOMON AND THE BIRDS.

KING Solomon commanded all Birds who
were his subjects to go forth to hunt for
food and to return everyone of them together at
nightfall. And in the evening when he had called
his subjects together again, the Eagle, one of his
own Body-guard, was found to be missing. Then
King Solomon commanded enquiry to be made,
"On what errand went this comrade of yours?"
And the most of them made reply, "He went on
no errand; he simply neglected to accompany us."
"If that is the case," spake the King, "he is nothing
but a rebel, and wherever you meet him, you are to
cut him down without question asked." On hearing
this, however, the Blue Heron made answer and
said, "Assuredly he went on some errand or other;
I crave one day's respite" (said he). And a like
reply was made by the Woodpecker, saying, "If he

64

had done any wrong, I should be the first person
to know of it. Am I not one of your Majesty's
Body-guard, and could I not settle it if he *had* done
any wrong? I crave two days' respite" (said he).
But the Thrush said only, "I crave three days."
So Solomon the King granted three days' respite.
Now when the days of respite were ended, the
Eagle returned and sought his comrades. And he
took counsel with the Woodpecker and persuaded
him to enter King Solomon's presence.

Then the Woodpecker went in before the King,
and made obeisance, and said, "The Eagle, your
Majesty, did not return the other day because he
found in a cavern of the rocks a follower of Her
Highness the daughter of the King of the Genii,
who is a person of surpassing beauty and worthy to
become a consort of your Majesty." To this the
King replied, "Very well, if you are strong enough to
do so, take her from him, you have our permission."
But the Eagle had arranged with the Woodpecker
to excavate a hollow in a tree, and they had put
the Princess in the hollow and closed the aperture
with pitch and the Eagle had mounted guard there.
So when the King heard this he said, "Bring

them both here, and I will grant his life." Then the Eagle brought the Princess before King Solomon, and the King commanded the Queen to make a lather of powdered rice and wash it off the Princess's person again with limes. At this the Princess's feathers disappeared and the white markings of her skin showed up in all their beauty. Thus the daughter of the King of the Genii was married unto Solomon the King.

Now when all these things had happened, King Solomon spake unto the assembled Birds and said, "If ye had had nothing to say, ye should have spoken like the Thrush. If ye had aught to say, ye should have spoken like the Blue Heron." And he cursed all the other birds with a great curse. And that is why to this day there are birds of so many different sorts, some with too long a beak, and others with too long a tail, and yet others with a black mark round the neck.

THE OUTWITTING OF THE GĔDÉMBAI.

THERE was formerly a race of gigantic spirits named Gĕdémbai who could turn people whom they addressed by name into wood or stone. Many years ago they were very numerous and were a great danger to the forest-dwelling Malays. In many places there are still to be seen the clearest traces of their former presence and power. Near the headwaters of the Tembĕling close to the left bank of the river stands a rock on which are still shown the claw-marks of a tiger, which escaped from the Gĕdémbai by leaping the river (where it was ten fathoms across), when a wild boar which it was pursuing was turned into stone. There to

67

this day you may see the Petrified Boar, and the place is known by the name of the Tiger's Leap. Further down the river stands a high and solitary crag, the summit of which is the shelter where the Gĕdémbai used to dry by day the fish they had caught during the previous night. There too you may see the big river-pool into which they threw their casting net, and the rocks which they dropped into the river (in place of the stones thrown in to attract the fish before the cast is made with the net).

Such was the havoc wrought by the Gĕdémbai that the older inhabitants at length conspired together to frighten them out of the land. For the Gĕdémbai were incredible fools, and could be cheated with great facility. And as they only went abroad at night, the Malays used certain stratagems to frighten the Gĕdémbai out of the country.

Pulling down the long weeping sprays of bamboo that overhung the streams, they cut them off short, and then let them spring back again to an upright position, so that the Gĕdémbai might think that only giants could have reached up to cut them.

68

Next they put an old man upwards of sixty years of age in a child's swinging cot, so that the Gĕdémbai seeing his toothless gums supposed him to be a new-born infant. And when the Gĕdémbai had thus been thoroughly cheated, they were easily made to believe that the harrows lying beside the rice-fields were Malay hair-combs, and that the very tortoises were insects that infested their persons; but that nevertheless they could make themselves small enough to creep inside the sheath of a dagger in order to hollow it out.

At length therefore the Gĕdémbai lost heart, and fled to the Country at the Foot of the Sky, but as they fled they called upon everybody they met to follow after them, turning all who refused to obey them into trees. Hence you will see in Malayan forests many lofty trees leaning over rivers. These were once men and women who refused to follow the Gĕdémbai in their flight, and were so severely kicked by them in consequence, that they have never since been able to stand upright. Here and there you will see trees whose silvery outer bark peels off in strips. These too, which are now

Pahlawan trees, were once human beings, but were transformed into trees for refusing to follow the Gĕdémbai, who caused their bark to fall off in patches by stroking the skin of their own breasts.

THE FATE OF THE SILVER PRINCE
AND PRINCESS LEMON-GRASS.

ONCE upon a time there was a beautiful king's daughter called Princess 'Lemon-grass'[1] who was betrothed to another king's son called the 'Silver' Prince[2]. In due course of time a lucky day for the wedding was fixed, and on its arrival the Bridegroom's party went forth in procession to escort him to the house of the Bride, with the noise of gongs and drums, according to the custom of the country. But at the very last hour, even while the Bridegroom's procession was approaching, the Bride changed her mind, and threatened to resist the Bridegroom by force. At this juncture however, one Těgah made peace between them, standing like a wall between the

[1] Sěrei.
[2] Pērak.

pair and forbidding the conflict. Yet even as they stood, they were all summoned by the Gĕdembai, and as they did not obey the summons, they were forthwith changed into Hills. And the name of the Hill into which the Princess was changed was 'Lemon-grass Crag[1]' (or 'Kedah Peak'), and that of the Prince was 'Silver Mountain[2],' and that of the peace-maker was 'Sheer Hill[3].' And so to this day 'Sheer Hill' stands like a wall between the conflicting parties.

[1] Gunong Jĕrai.
[2] Bukit Pērak.
[3] Bukit Tĕgah.

NOTES.

P. 1 1.   Father Lime-stick and the Flower-pecker.

This tale, which appears in England as early as the *Gesta Romanorum* (ch. 167), was told me by a Kelantan Malay named Che Busu, one of the following of the Raja Muda of Patāni. The liming of birds as practised by the Malays is effected by cutting deep notches in the boughs of any tree in which birds have been observed to habitually settle, the operator inserting in each notch a short stick thickly coated with viscid sap obtained from certain trees in the jungle. When the birds have been caught these lime-sticks can be removed and used afresh in a different locality, this being much less trouble than it would be to lime the twigs of the tree itself.

Some of these lime-sticks in the Cambridge Museum are about 2 ft. in length, and of rather less than the thickness of the little finger.

The Malay name of the old man in the present instance is 'To' Să-gĕtah,' the Malay name of the bird being 'Sĕpah putri' or the 'Princess's betel-quid,' a name which is derived from another legend.   "The Owl fell in love with the Moon-Princess and asked her to marry him. This she promised to do, if he would allow her to finish her quid of betel undisturbed, but before finishing it she threw it down to the earth, where it took the form of the small bird in question. The Princess then requested the Owl to make search for it, but as, of course, he was unable to find it, the proposed match fell through. This is the reason why the owl, to quote the Malay proverb, 'sighs longingly to the moon,' and is the type of the desponding lover." *Malay Magic*, 102.

1 12. **A Bezoar-stone as big as a coconut.** These Bezoar-stones are concretions obtained from the bodies of various animals, especially the porcupine and the monkey. Extraordinary magical virtues are ascribed to them. They are usually about the size of a small filbert (more or less), and their value, all else being equal, would be in proportion to their size. In the *Gesta Romanorum* (above referred to), it is a " Pearl bigger than the egg of an ostrich."

1 13. **worth at least a thousand** : i.e. a thousand dollars, the dollar being about two shillings.

P. 3 1. **The King of the Tigers is sick.**
This story was also one of Che Busu's.

3 18. **because of a dream of certain medicine.** It is hardly necessary to remind the reader of the extraordinary importance assigned to dreams by all uncivilised races.

P. 5 1. **The Mouse-deer's shipwreck.**
This again was one of the tales told me by Che Busu.

5 5. Of the bird which I have translated Heron all I could ascertain was that it was a species of Heron distinguished by the roundness of its tail-parts. The Malays call it burong kuntul [in Patāni and Kelantan 'kutu'].

5 6. **the wind blew from the North.** This would of course be a most favourable wind for anyone who wanted to sail to Java from any part of the Malay Peninsula.

6 1. **I'm such a bad hand at swimming.** The thin legs and deeply cloven hoofs of the Mouse-deer would be sufficient in themselves to account for this.

8 7. **climbed up with it to the top of a She-oak tree.** The She-oak is the name given (I believe) in Australia to *Casuarina litorea* or the 'long-shore' casuarina-tree. The

Notes

name of she-oak was given to this tree on account of the wood which was thought to resemble oak in appearance though it was really hardly fit even for fire-wood. It has needle-like leaves, and hence from a distance looks very like fir or larch. It is to be found as a rule in the Malay Peninsula wherever there is a sandy sea-board. The Malays call it 'Ru (short for Aru or Ĕru) which name they also apply to a kind of fir which grows in the mountains.

P. 9 1. **Who killed the Otter's Babies?**

This is another of Che Busu's Tales, but when he told it me there was a missing link, that of the king-crab, which he could not recollect. As, however, I heard the story re-told and the link supplied in Kedah, I take the opportunity of making good the omission. The Malay word 'anak' may mean either 'child' or children, according to the context, but as in this context it is impossible to tell whether the singular or the plural is intended, I have thought it best, the Otter being a fairly prolific animal, to keep to the plural. In either case, however, it does not affect the point of the tale.

The otter is, so far as I am aware, much the same as the common otter (*Lutra vulgaris*).

The tale is of a kind which may perhaps best be called an all-round-the-clock or more simply a 'clock' story, as it ingeniously sets forth the chain of incidents, by which the responsibility for the death of its own children was brought home to the Otter itself, thanks to the wisdom of king Solomon, who here figures, as in so many other Eastern fables, as a judge of extraordinary discretion.

P. 11 4. **the Woodpecker...sounded the war-gong**: this of course is an allusion to the tapping of the woodpecker's bill upon the bark of tree-trunks in its search for insects.

11 15. **the Great Lizard wearing his sword.** The Great Lizard is the "Iguana," as it is often called (more correctly, the Monitor Lizard of the Far East). It grows to an immense size, even reaching a length of more than six feet. From three to

75

five feet however is the common size. The Great Lizard's sword is of course the long and tapering tail which he trails behind him.

P. 12 2. **the Tortoise had donned his coat of mail.** This refers clearly enough to the mail-like shell by which the tortoise is protected. The expression here used is a favourite paraphrase such as with the Malays often takes the form of a riddle. "An old hunchback wearing a coat of mail armour; What is it?" the answer being of course "A tortoise": most of the paraphrases referred to in this tale are also I believe known to the Malays in the form of riddles.

12 6. **the King-crab trailing his three-edged pike.** The king-crab is a *limulus*. The pike here referred to is a bayonet-shaped spike which (like our own "Morning Star") was specially used in former times by the Malays for piercing chain-armour. Hence it is here employed as usually, in conjunction with the armour. The allusion in this instance is to the curious spike at the end of the king-crab's tail.

12 10. **the Crayfish had shouldered his lance.** The Malay word may either signify crayfish, in which case it belongs to the family of the Astacidæ, the 'lance' being an allusion to the crayfish's long feelers or antennæ when turned backwards over its shoulder; or else it may mean prawn, in which case it probably refers to the fretted spike or saw on the prawn's head. The word used for lance in the Malay refers to the fringed or tasselled lance which is used in many parts of the Far East as one of the insignia of royalty, and which is decorated, in various localities, with yak or cow-tails, with horse-hair &c. &c.

P. 13 1. **A Vegetarian Dispute.**

This story was taken down on the banks of the Upper Tĕmbĕling River, in the interior of Pahang. As the object of the last tale was to explain in a playful (semi-serious, semi-comic) vein the origin of the most striking characteristics of certain animals, so the present story attempts to account for the chief characteristics of certain objects in the vegetable world.

76

Notes

Unfortunately I have not, in two or three cases, been able to identify the plant, though the general tenour of the story is perfectly clear. The identifications which follow are taken from a list of Malay plants by H. N. Ridley in *J. R. A. S.*, S. B. [No. 30], July, 1897.

13 2. **Jágong** is the Malay name for Indian Corn or Maize, which is largely grown as a 'catch'-crop in the Malay Peninsula.

13 5. **Dăgun** is a *Gnetum*, probably *edule*.

Gădong is *Dioscorea dæmonum* Roxb. (Dioscoreaceæ). It is a climber with large tubers, which are used in the manufacture of dart-poison, and also eaten after repeated washings to extract the narcotic properties which they contain.

13 11. **Káchang** may here be any kind of cultivated bean, such as is grown (in company with maize) as a 'catch'-crop.

13 14. Libut, the tree so called in Pahang (also Bĕlibok in Ulu Kelantan), is almost certainly the "Kĕlĕbok" tree of the W. coast (Selangor &c.). It is a species of Ficus (? *F. Roxburghii*, Wall., Urticaceæ), a large ficus, "with clusters of big figs on the stem." It is a light wood, used by the wild tribes for making the butts of their blow-gun darts.

P. 14 6. The Liane referred to is a kind of creeper called Wilang (unidentified).

14 14. The "Ox-eye tree" (māta lémbu) is also unmentioned in the Dictionaries.

14 17. The Pĕráchak (also Pĕrachek and Pĕrachet) is *Tabernæmontana Malaccensis*, Hook. fil. (Apocynaceæ).

14 21. "And'ram" is also unmentioned, but may probably be taken as a dialectal variation of mĕndĕrong, a common kind of sedge used in mat-making. (*Scirpus grossus*, Vahl. Cyperaceæ.)

P. 16 1. **The Friendship of Tŭpai the Squirrel and Rŭan the Creeping Fish.**

This tale was told me as a proverbial example of devoted friendship, by one of the local Malays at a village on the banks of the Siong River, a long way up-country in the State of Kedah.

The Squirrel is the common striped squirrel of the Malay Peninsula, and the Fish is an 'ophiocephalus,' a kind of swamp-fish that is able both to walk and climb by opening and shutting its gill-cases. I have here called it the creeping fish to distinguish it from the walking mud-fish of Africa, the point of the story in the present case being moreover its ability to creep out of the tube; but it is best known locally for its walking powers, of which I have myself been a witness.

16 12. **a bamboo water-tube.** These water-tubes are the so-called joints (or inter-nodes) of a big species of bamboo with long inter-nodes. They are often as much as 5 ft. to 6 ft. in length (by 4 or 5 inches in diameter); and when I was at Siong (where this story was collected), I used regularly to see (in the early morning) the women of the hamlet carrying them down to the water and refilling them there. They are used by jungle Malays, I believe, throughout the Peninsula.

16 18. Nesting-places for the hens are often made at the top of similar bamboos, the upper end of the tube being split in many places all round and opened out in the form of a basket, which is lined and filled with a little earth, forming a species of nest for the hen to roost in. Like the water-bamboos they are usually kept close to the house.

P. 18 1. **The Pelican's punishment.**

This is a Malay version of one of the best-known of Æsop's Fables. It was collected on the Tĕmbĕling river in Ulu Pahang.

P. 20 1. **The Tiger gets his deserts.**

As my friend Mr R. J. Wilkinson points out, this tale occurs in the Hikayat Gul Bakhtiyar. It was collected in Ulu Kedah (Siong).

P. 22 1. **The Tiger's mistake.**

This is one of the Tĕmbĕling Stories, and was told me as having happened on the very spot (upon the banks of the Lĕbih

Notes

River) on which I was one night encamped. The spot was a small point of land jutting out into the stream of the Lĕbih which swirled angrily past, chafing at the steep bank which here disputed its passage. It was surrounded by a dense wall of jungle and it appeared just the place to expect a tiger, although it may be open to question whether crocodiles are ever met so far up-stream and above so many rapids.

P. 24 1. **The Tune that makes the Tiger drowsy.**

This Tune which the Malays call "*Lāgu rīmau mĕngántok*" may perhaps only exist in the popular imagination, like our own "tune the cow died of." The phrase appears to be pretty generally known in the East Coast States, though I had not heard it in the States of the Western Sea-board. The 'kĕrōtong' is a 'joint' of bamboo, longitudinal strips of the skin of which are raised with a knife, and tightened by means of wedges (or 'bridges') inserted (under the strips) at both ends, so that the strips form the instrument's strings. The strings may be two or more in number, and are twanged with the fingers.

P. 26 1. **The Tigers' Fold.**

The scene of this story is laid in the district of Ulu Sĕtiu, in the East-Coast Malay State of Trenggānu. The story of the Tigers' Fold is a favourite subject with Malay story-tellers, the Fold being usually described as situated upon any neighbouring hill or mountain of considerable height, *e.g.* Gunong Ledang or Mount Ophir, a well-known mountain in the interior of Malacca territory (about 4000 ft.).

P. 28 1. **The Tiger and the Shadow.**

This tale is from Ulu Kedah. It is an interesting Malay version of our own "Dog and the Shadow."

28 2. The 'salt-licks' of the Malay Peninsula (called *Sira* in Kedah and *Jĕnut* in Ulu Pahang) are famous places for big game. They are places where the ground is thickly saturated with natural salts derived usually from the overflowing of hot mineral springs in the vicinity.

28 12. **Kuwis** is the smallest of the Malay flying squirrels, and is not much larger than our own common bat.

P. 30 1. **Wit wins the day.**

This story is new to me; it was told me by a Kelantan Malay.

P. 31 23. **he kept trying to clamber on to the raft.** In the upper reaches of rivers in many of the East-Coast (Malay) States it is the custom to keep bamboo rafts moored under the steep banks, instead of the fallen tree-trunks which more commonly form the landing-stages of the West-Coast Malays.

P. 33 1. **The King-crow and the Water-snail.**

This story is an old friend in a new dress. It was told me on the Tĕmbĕling River by a Malay of Pahang. The King-crow (also called the Racquet-tailed Drongo) is the "Chenchawi" of the Malays, and the Water-snail is "Siput."

P. 34 9. **Birah** is a name given to various wild aroids.

Kĕmahang seems to be a *Dioscorea*.

34 21. It is a common Malay belief that many species of shell-fish (*e.g.* when the tide is coming up) make audible sounds, which the Malays usually describe as 'whistling.' A similar superstition appears to have once been current in England, witness the portrayal of "The Whistling Oyster" on the sign-boards of old inns.

P. 38 1. **The Elephant Princess.**

This tale, which I picked up in Patāni, is obscure in parts, but shows distinct traces of Siamese influence (*e.g.* in the mention of the Siamese (Buddhist) Monastery). There are many of these monasteries in the State of Patāni, inhabited by the yellow-robed priests of Buddha.

38 2. The 'Prophet' Adam and the 'Lady Eve' (Baba Hawa) are the usual titles assigned by the Malays to the traditional ancestors of mankind. For a parallel story, see *Malay Magic*, p. 151 seqq.

38 7. **making a bridge of a soap-vine stem.** This refers to the Malay soap-vine called Bĕluru; [the only one given in

80

Notes

Ridley's List being *Entada scandens* L. (Leguminosæ)], short pieces of whose stem are broken up and mixed with water, which is then worked up into a lather and used for washing purposes by Jungle-dwelling Malays, in place of soap. It is a fairly big and strong creeper.

P. 39 12. **scooped out the contents of a giant gourd.** This recalls the state carriage (in our own story of Cinderella) which was improvised out of a pumpkin.

39 19. **his iron pike-head**; this is a pike called " sā " (sau), such as is carried by elephant-drivers.

P. 41 1. **The Elephant's bet.**
This story was told me by Che Busu, the Kĕlantan Malay already referred to.

P. 45 5. **went to look for it at the house of a maker of palm-wine.** Palm-wine or toddy is made by tapping the big fleshy flower-shoot (axis) of the coconut-palm; the sap is run off into short bamboo vessels and allowed to ferment (when required for drinking purposes) or boiled down to make a kind of molasses or palm-sugar as required.

P. 49 1. **Princess Sādong of the Caves.**
This story (from Kedah) seems to be widely known in the Malay Peninsula, in most places at all events where there are lime-stone hills and hill-goats (Kambing gurun), the name of Princess Sādong being commonly invoked by way of diverting the hill-goats from the crops. It also turns up in the Islands (of the Malay Archipelago) as the Story of the Princess who refused all her Suitors. The Country of What-you-will is called in Malay " Alang-ka-suka," or " Alang-'kau-suka."

P. 50 18. **the Prince who was born in the Foam.** In "The Story of Patāni" it is the Princess who is rescued from the Foam and the Prince who is discovered in the stem of the Big Bamboo. Such local variations are very common, each district having its own way of telling what it regards as its own story. See however the notes to the "Story of Patāni."

Notes

P. 52 1. **The Saint that was shot out of his own cannon.**

This curious legend was told me by Mula Awang, of Patāni.

52 17. **Grésik**, now a mere hamlet some three or four miles from Patāni town, was once the seat of royalty here, but has evidently been many years abandoned. I was shown the spot upon which the cannon (out of which Che Long was fired) is said to have stood, my Malay companion drawing my attention to the fact that it was bare of grass, since none would grow there after the event here described.

52 18. **Kuála Bárat** or the Western River-mouth is an old mouth of the Patāni river (now silted up).

P. 53 4. **The Luck of Patāni** (Mal., Sri Patāni). I believe a small cannon bearing this name is to be seen in the Museum at Bangkok.

P. 54 1. **The story of the Saints whose Grave-stones moved.**

This story was from the same source as the last. Father Lanky's real name was, I was told, Seh (= Sheikh?) Rombok.

P. 55 3. **Jámbu** is the chief town of the Jĕring District; it lies a few miles S. E. from Patāni Town.

P. 56. I myself paid a visit to the tombs of the two saints and was requested to try my fortune, all the neighbouring villagers turning out to watch the proceedings. The two graves, which were protected by a low wall and a roof, had been made, I found, in the sand, and were covered by long low mounds of sand from head to foot. This circumstance, combined with the fact that the measuring instrument was a short stick (supposed to be a cubit long, corresponding exactly to the length of the operator's arm as measured from elbow to middle finger tip), made the task a harder one than might have been expected. Each time a cubit was measured, a furrow was made in the sand to mark the place, and the loose sand falling in on both sides of the furrow, it was by no means easy to be sure of the exact centre of the furrow when the next cubit came to be measured. Fortu-

82

Notes

nately however, in my own case, the error came out on the right side, as the second measurement came to a little more than the first; a result on which I was warmly congratulated by my Malay friends.

P. 57 1. **Nakhōda Rágam.**

There are many versions of this story in various parts of the Peninsula, this particular one being told me in Patāni. Nakhōda is a Persian word (meaning Ship-master) which has been borrowed by the Malays. "Nakhōda Rágam," it appears, was the familiar name of one "Sultan Bulkeiah" of Borneo, described in Bornean traditions as a great warrior and a great navigator, he having voyaged to Java and Malacca, and conquered the East Coast of Borneo, Luzon and Suluk. His wife, called Lela Men Chanei, was a daughter of the Batara of Suluk. —Hugh Low on the Selesilah of the Rajas of Brunei, *J. R. A. S.*, S.B. no. 5, p. 7 (notes).

57 5. **Jĕring** is the name of the District of which Jámbu (*v.* supra) is the chief town.

P. 58 4. **Bánggor** is a name given to any knoll of rising ground or low eminence near a river, and in this case it probably refers to the site of Jámbu village.

P. 59 1. **The Legend of Patāni.**

This story, which is a well-known Malay legend, and which purports to describe the first beginnings of the State of Patāni, was told me by a Malay in Patāni Town.

59 4. **Nang Cháyang** is the name of an early queen of Patāni.

59 12. For this Foam Princess, cp. Malay Annals (trans. by Leyden, London 1821) p. 29: "It happened on a certain day "that the river of Palembang brought down a foam-bell of "uncommon size, in which appeared a young girl of extreme "beauty. The Raja being informed of this circumstance, ordered "her to be brought to him. This was done, and the Raja adopted "her as his daughter. She was named Putri Tunjong-bui, or the "Princess Foam-bell." Palembang is in Sumatra.

P. 61 4. **he found a male infant.** In many versions the two children—the Bamboo Prince and the Foam Princess—are made to marry when they grow up.

61 12. **The Rājas of Rāman who may not eat the young bamboo shoots.** From this it may perhaps be inferred that the Bamboo was their totem. The traces of genuine totemism among the Peninsular Malays are however of the rarest description.

P. 66 4. **a lather of powdered rice.** The Malay method of (ceremonial) bathing is to cover the person with a lather made of finely powdered rice mixed with various other substances, and to wash it off again with the juice of limes.

P. 67 1. **The Outwitting of the Gĕdémbai.**
This class of spirits is usually called *K'lembai*, but as this tale is from Ulu Pahang (Tĕmbĕling River) I have retained the local form of the name. I quote in conclusion an interesting note from the *J. R. A. S.* by the late Sir William Maxwell, which runs as follows:—

"sperti bujuk lĕpas deri bubu.

"Like a 'bujuk' fish escaped from the trap.

"Bujuk is a fresh-water fish found in muddy plaçes. Bubu "is a fish-trap made of split bamboo tied with rattan. It has a "circular opening which narrows as the end of the passage is "reached and is constructed on the same principle as the eel-pot "or lobster-pot. One of the highest mountains in Perak is called "Bubu. It is supposed to be the fish-trap of the mythological "personage named Sang Kalembai, and the rocks in the bed of "the Perak river at Pachat are pointed out as his Sawar (stakes "which are put down to obstruct a stream and thus to force "the fish to take the opening which leads to the trap)."

[Maxwell in *J. R. A. S.*, S. B. no. 1, p. 145.]

P. 68 9. This is a common Malay practice for netting fresh-water fish. The stones thrown in are called " Batu Tungkul."

P. 70 1. **Pahlawan** = *Tristania whitiana*, a striking tree in Malayan forests. Its bark peels off in strips.

P. 71 4. **Princess Lemon-grass.** By a popular etymology,

84

Notes

the Malay name of Kedah Peak (" Gūnong Jĕrai" or "'Jĕrai' Crag") is here derived from the Malay word sĕrei which means 'lemon-grass' (citronella). In the "Hikayat Marong Maha-wangsa" it is said to be so called "on account of its height." The name is however undoubtedly taken from the name of the Tree (Jĕrai), v. *supra* (p. 36).

71 6. **the Silver Prince.** The Malay word for silver is " Perak," whence not only the name of this mountain, but also those of the Perak river and the Perak state, are derived.

P. 72 7. **Sheer Hill.** This is the meaning of the name of " Būkit Tĕgah," a steep hill situated between the Silver Mountain (Būkit Perak) and Kedah Peak (Gūnong Jĕrai). I may add that the difference in use of the terms "Gūnong" and " Būkit" has nothing whatever to do with the question of height (as in the case of the words 'hill' and 'mountain' in English). The former (gūnong) means a more or less bare and precipitous peak or crag, whilst the latter (būkit) is used of all forest-covered hills or mountains.

Note on Pronunciation.

The spelling followed is that of Standard (Peninsular) Malay, romanised according to the sound of the Italian vowels. *J, Ch,* and other consonants here used, (except final *K*), roughly speaking, as in English. Final *K* is a strong guttural check, *G* always hard. *NG* is a single letter, and hence *NGG* has to be used to express the sound of *NG* in Eng. "longer," "stronger," &c.

85

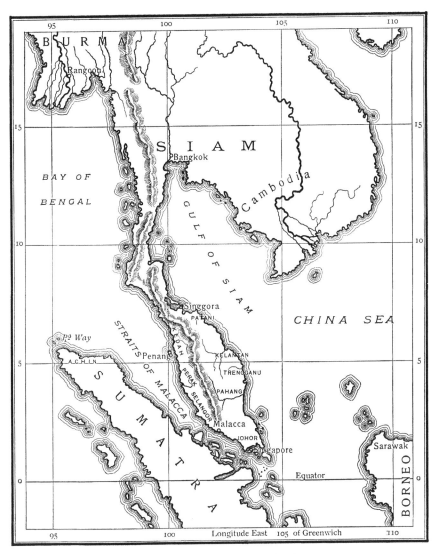

X. MAP OF MALAY PENINSULA.

INDEX.

Index

Index

S. 12

Index